Traditional Scottish Recipes

Traditional Scottish Recipes

Written out in manuscript form by George L. Thomson, scribe

Canongate

Pentalic/Taplinger

1978

First published in 1976 by Canongate Publishing Ltd.
17 Jeffrey Street, Edinburgh
Second Impression 1977
Paperback Edition 1978

©

1976
George L Thomson
ISBN 0 903937 64 6

First published in the U.S.A in 1978 by Pentalic /Taplinger
200 Park Avenue South
New York 10003
ISBN D 8008 7019 0

Printed and bound in Great Britain by T.&A. Constable Ltd.
Hopetoun Street, Edinburgh

Introduction

Some years ago a friend suggested that traditional Scottish recipes would be a good subject for a book. Eventually I had enough to write this book, which was for my own use and pleasure, though as a calligrapher I had it in mind some day to try to sell it to some rich buyer. People who saw it in its unbound state thought I should have it published. It seemed to me it would be a splendid thing if the book could be shared by thousands instead of being locked away in the library of one person; so I was delighted when the publishers accepted it, and even more so when it sold so well.

My mother, who was "in service" from the time she left school until she married in 1915, was a good cook and baker, and I remember used many of these recipes. No mass-produced haggis or tinned soup could ever compete with her Haggis or Sheep's Heid Broth!

I intend that this should be an enjoyable book to look at; but I hope some of the fascinating titles will encourage you to prepare and savour some of the delicious foods appreciated in Scotland for generations.

Ye Pow'rs wha mak mankind your care,
And dish them out their bill of fare,
Auld Scotland wants nae skinkin ware
    That jaups in luggies;
But, if ye wish her gratefu' pray'r,
    Gie her a Haggis!

ROBERT BURNS

Haggis

1 lb lean mutton · sheep's stomach · lights, liver &
heart [pluck] · 2 cups oatmeal · 4 onions · ¼ lb suet ·
pepper and salt

Wash the stomach bag thoroughly in salted
water. Boil the pluck for 1½ hours, leaving
the windpipe attached and hanging
out of the pot so that impurities may
pass out. When cooked and cold, cut
away the windpipe and any skin or
gristle. Reserving some of the lights,
mince the pluck with the mutton & suet.
Toast the oatmeal and chop the onions.
Herbs may be added as preferred. Mix
in a bowl the minced ingredients, oatmeal,
onions, herbs, pepper & salt with about
a pint of the stock in which the pluck
was boiled, to a soft consistency. Take
the stomach bag and spoon in the mixture
until rather more than half full [to
allow room for the meal to expand]. Sew

Use coarse or "pin-head" oatmeal

1

up firmly, prick thoroughly, and tie
in a cloth. Place in a pan of boiling
water with a plate in the bottom and
boil for three or four hours. Prick
occasionally to prevent bursting. Serve
with champit tatties and neeps.

* * *

Stovies

Potatoes · butter or dripping · onions · salt · pepper

The potatoes if new should be all the same
size; if old, cut to even sized pieces.
Peel and put into a saucepan with not
more than ½" of water. Season to taste.
Clean salt water, if obtainable, imparts
a unique flavour. Dot generously with
butter, cover tightly and simmer gently
until cooked. Check after 30 minutes,
and shake occasionally to prevent sticking.
An alternative method is to fry two sliced

2

onions in dripping until lightly browned.
Add thickly sliced potatoes with water
& seasoning, and cook as before, omitting
the butter. The floury varieties of potatoes
are best for stovies. New potatoes are
delicious if, when ready, a handful of
oatmeal is sifted over them. Replace
the lid and shake well, then leave on
the side of the stove for 10 minutes. Serve
hot, with glasses of ice-cold buttermilk.

* * *

Tattie Scones

½ lb boiled potatoes · 2 oz flour · ½ oz butter · ¼ tsp salt

Mash the potatoes with the butter, then
thoroughly mix in the flour and salt.
Roll out thinly, cut in four and fire both
sides on a hot girdle. Cool on a towel.

* * *

Mealy Pudden

1 lb oatmeal · ½ lb chopped suet · 2 onions · pepper and
salt

Chop the onions and mix all the ingredients
together. Tie up loosely in a scalded
cloth, leaving ample room to swell. Boil
for 2 hours. Broth or soup may be used
instead of plain water. If steamed in a
bowl, allow about 3 hours. May be served
with meat or by itself.

* * *

Tattie Soup

2 lbs potatoes · ½ lb onions · ½ lb carrots · 1 tsp sugar·
3 quts bone stock· salt and pepper

Stock from roast mutton bones makes very
good potato soup, as does tripe stock, but
if none is available, use 1 lb neck of mutton.

Start the bones or meat in cold water or
stock, and bring slowly to the boil, removing
any scum. Simmer for 1 hour. Peel &
slice the potatoes, chop the onions & grate
the carrots; add to the stock with the sugar
and seasoning, & bring again to the boil.
Simmer steadily for 1½ hours. A tasty
addition in season is a handful of young
nettle tops, finely chopped and added
10 minutes before the soup is served.

* * *

Buttery Rowies

1 lb flour · 8 oz butter · 4 oz lard · ¾ pt tepid water ·
1 oz yeast or ½ tblsp dried yeast · 1 tblsp sugar · salt

Mix the sifted flour with a pinch of salt
into a warm basin. Cream the yeast with
the sugar, and when working, add with
the tepid water to the flour. Mix well.
Cover & leave in a warm place for 30 minutes,

or until it has doubled its size. Cream together the butter and lard, then divide in three portions. Roll out the dough on a floured board into a long strip. Dot ⅓ of the creamed fats over the top third of the strip, and fold over & roll out as when making flaky pastry. Repeat with the rest of the fat. Then roll out and cut into small ovals or rounds. Place on a floured baking sheet, leaving at least 2" space between to allow for swelling. Cover and leave to rise for 45 minutes. Bake in a moderate to hot oven for 20 minutes.

* * *

Girdle Scones

1 lb flour · 2 tsp cream of tartar · 1 tsp baking soda · ½ tsp salt · milk

Sour or buttermilk is best, in which case use only 1 teaspoon of cream of tartar. Mix

flour and dry ingredients. Add milk to
make a soft dough. Handle as little as
possible. Place on a floured board, roll out
and cut out scones with a cutter. Bake
on a hot girdle.

* * *

Shortbread

1 lb flour · ¾ lb rice flour · 1 lb butter · ½ lb caster
sugar · ½ tsp salt

Cream together the butter and sugar.
Mix in the flour and rice flour, with
the salt, until the texture is similar to
short crust pastry mixture. Press firmly
by hand into two round baking tins.
It is not necessary to grease them first.
Do not knead, as this will give too heavy
a texture to your shortbread. Make a
decorative border with finger and thumb,
or use the handle end of a tablespoon.

7

Prick all over with a fork. Bake in a
moderate oven for about one hour.
Allow to cool before turning out on to
a wire tray. Ground rice may be
substituted for the rice flour.

* * *

Baps

1 lb flour. 2 oz lard · 1 oz yeast · 1 tsp sugar · 1 tsp salt.
½ pint tepid milk

Cream together the yeast and sugar.
Mix the flour and salt in a warm bowl.
Melt the lard, adding about half the tepid
milk. Make a well in the flour, and into
it put the remaining milk, the yeast &
the lard, and mix well by hand or with a
wooden spoon. Knead smooth, sprinkle with
flour, cover & leave to rise for 60 minutes. Then
knead lightly on a floured board. Form
into ovals 3"x2". Place on a baking sheet,

and brush with milk; but if preferred,
dust with flour only.   Leave to rise for 15
minutes, then make a small dent in the middle
of each with your finger.   Bake in a hot
oven for 15 to 20 minutes.

* * *

Howtowdie

4 lb roasting chicken · 6 small onions or shallots · 4oz butter
chicken's liver · 1 pt giblet stock · 2 tblsp thick cream · 2 cloves
6 black peppercorns · 2 lbs spinach · pinch of mace · salt
pepper. STUFFING · 2oz fresh breadcrumbs · 1 chopped
small shallot · 1 tsp chopped tarragon · 1 tsp chopped
parsley · milk · salt · pepper

Soak the breadcrumbs in just enough milk
to soften & make them swell. Add the rest
of the stuffing ingredients, mix well and
put inside the fowl. Use a small skewer to
close. Put the butter in a casserole, saving
1 level tablespoon, and heat. Add the onions,

and when lightly browned, put in the
chicken. Roast for 20 minutes in a hot
oven, turning frequently till lightly browned,
then add mace, cloves, seasoning and the
boiling stock. Cover and cook in a moderate
oven until done, about 40 minutes. The
spinach should meanwhile be cooked, well
drained, and kept hot. When the fowl
is taken from the oven, strain the stock
into a saucepan, add the chopped liver &
cook gently for 5 minutes, then mash the
liver into the stock. Add the remaining
butter and the cream and heat again without
boiling. Put the drained and seasoned
spinach round the edges of an oval dish.
place chicken in the centre. Pour the sauce
over it, but not over the spinach.
"Howtowdie wi'Drappit Eggs" is made by poaching
eggs in the stock before adding the liver.
Keep them warm on the hot spinach before
serving.

* * *

Syllabub

1 pt cream · juice of 2 lemons · ½ lb sugar · 1 glass of sherry

Whisk all the ingredients together thoroughly until stiff. Put into glasses and allow to stand 12 hours before serving.

* * *

Het Pint

4 pts light ale · ½ pt whisky · ¼ lb sugar · 3 eggs

Add to the ale in a stout pan about a teaspoonful of ground nutmeg and slowly heat, but avoid bringing to the boil. Stir in the sugar until melted. Then very slowly stir in the thoroughly beaten eggs, with the pan off the heat. This should prevent curdling. Now add the whisky and re-heat; again do not boil. Pouring your Het Pint several

times into heated containers will clear &
brighten the brew.

* * *

Pirr

4 tblsp oatmeal · 1 pt water · 2 tsp sugar · ½ tsp cream
of tartar · milk

In a warm jug, mix well the oatmeal, sugar
[brown sugar is best], and cream of tartar.
Add enough cold milk to make a smooth
paste. Stir well while pouring in the boiling
water. This hot beverage from Shetland is
also esteemed as a cure for colds when taken
before going to bed.

* * *

Barm Loaf

1 lb oatmeal · 1 tblsp flour · 1 tblsp treacle [or syrup] ·
1 tsp baking soda · pepper · salt ·
buttermilk

Take enough buttermilk to make an easy
pouring batter with all the ingredients.
Pour this into a generously greased cake
tin, and bake in a slow oven for 60 minutes.

* * *

Clapshot

1 lb potatoes · ¾ lb turnip · 1 onion, chives, or shallots ·
1 oz butter or dripping · pepper · salt

Boil the turnip first for 15 or 20 minutes, then
add the potatoes & boil till cooked. Small
turnips can be put together with the potatoes.
Drain, add chopped onion and the other ingredients,
and mash together thoroughly. A larger

13

proportion of turnip may make the dish
too wet . Serve very hot with a meat course.

* * *

Petticoat Tails

12 oz flour · 4 oz butter · 4 oz caster sugar · 4 tblsp milk

Heat the milk and melt the butter into
it . Mix thoroughly with the flour and
sugar. Roll out into rounds, ¼" or less
thick, on a floured board. Use an egg-cup
or small cutter to cut a circle in the centre,
then cut straight lines from this to the edge,
to make 8 segments. Prick lightly with
a fork. Bake on greased tray for about 30
minutes in a slow oven. Sprinkle with
caster sugar while still hot, allow to cool
on a wire tray.
Some people like these with caraway seeds:
add ¼ oz to the mixture if you like them.

* * *

14

Dundee Marmalade

2 lb bitter oranges · 2 lemons · 8 lbs sugar · 7 pts water

Wash the fruit. Cut in halves & remove
the pips, which are left to soak in ½ pint
of water. Put the fruit through a coarse
cut mincer, or cut up by hand. Cover with
cold water in a basin & leave 24 hours. Then
tie the pips in a cloth, and boil with the
fruit and water for 1 hour. Add the sugar,
stirring until it boils, and boil for 45 minutes,
or until the marmalade jells when tested
in the usual way. Pour into warmed pots,
and cover at once.

* * *

Gruel

1 tblsp oatmeal · ½ pt water · pinch salt

Fine oatmeal is best for this. Soak the oatmeal

15

in the cold water for up to 30 minutes, then
use a spoon to press all the floury water from
it into a pan, leaving the oatmeal as dry
as possible. Add salt, and heat the liquor
until it boils, stirring continuously. Simmer
for about 20 minutes. Milk may be used
instead of water, or milk and water. A
taste of honey and / or whisky gives a
change of flavour.

* * *

Nettle Beer

3 handfuls nettle tops · 2 handfuls dandelion leaves ·
2 handfuls Sticky Wullie · sprig sage · 1 gal. water · 1 oz
dried yeast · 1 oz bruised ginger root · ½ oz cream of tartar

Add the nettles, dandelion, cleavers & sage to one
gallon of boiling water, boil 15 minutes,
then strain. Add * sugar and ginger and
boil a further 15 minutes. Strain again.
When lukewarm, put in a piece of toast

16   *   add about one pound of sugar

on which you have spread the creamed yeast.
Stir in the cream of tartar when fermentation
has stopped [this will take a varying number
of days, depending on the temperature.]
Skim surface, then bottle & firmly cork
the beer. Store the bottles on their sides
in a cool place. The beer may be used
in a few days time.

* * *

Abernethy Biscuits

½ lb flour · 3 oz butter · 3 oz caster sugar · 1 egg · 1½ tblsp
milk. ½ tsp baking pdr.

Rub the butter into the flour and sugar. Add
the baking powder. Mix in the egg and
milk, switched together. Roll out thinly
on a lightly floured board. Cut out in
biscuit rounds, prick with a fork, and
bake for 10 minutes in a moderate oven.

* * *

Cranachan

1 pint double cream · 1 cup oatmeal · caster sugar.
rum or vanilla

Lightly toast the oatmeal [use only coarse
oatmeal]. Beat the cream to a stiffish
froth, then stir in the oatmeal. You
may need less or more, depending how
thick you prefer it. Sweeten to taste, and
flavour with rum or vanilla. This sweet
is improved by the addition of fresh
berries in season.

* * *

Forfar Bridies

1 lb beefsteak · 3 oz suet · 1 onion · 1 lb flour · ¼ lb fat ·
½ pt water · salt & pepper

Mince the steak coarsely, season and
divide into three. Mix the flour & salt,

adding the boiling water and fat, and
when cool enough, turn the lump of dough
on to a floured board and knead well.
Divide and roll out thinly into three ovals.
Cover half each oval with meat, leaving a
margin round the edge for joining. Spread
minced suet and onion over the meat, wet
the edges of the pastry, fold over the top &
pinch all round with finger & thumb to join.
Make a small hole or slits in the top. Bake
in a quick oven about 30 minutes. Short
or puff pastry may be used if preferred).

* * *

Hatted Kit

2 pts buttermilk · 1–2 pints fresh milk · sugar · nutmeg ·
double cream

Just before milking time, warm up the buttermilk
and take it to the side of the cow. Milk
in about a pint, and stir well. Leave until

the next milking and repeat. Leave now
until the curd forms and grows the HAT.
Remove the curd & press the whey out
through a fine sieve until the curd is stiff
enough. Season to taste with sugar and
nutmeg, and serve with whipped cream.

* * *

Parlies *

1 lb flour. ½ lb butter. ½ lb brown sugar. ½ lb black
treacle. 2-4 tsp g. ginger

Cream together the butter and sugar, add
the flour, treacle and ground ginger, and
beat thoroughly. Drop in teaspoonfuls
on a greased tray, and bake for fifteen
to twenty minutes in a moderate oven.

* * *

* Parliament Cakes

20

Oatcakes

1 cup oatmeal · ¼ cup hot water · 1 tsp fat · ¼ tsp baking
soda · salt

Mix together the oatmeal, soda and a good
pinch of salt. Melt the fat in hot water
and add to make a soft paste. Put this
on baking board, sift oatmeal over it and
knead well until smooth. Roll out into
a round, very thinly, and cut into four
or six pieces. Brush off surplus meal and
bake on a hot girdle. Turn over when the
edges start to curl up. Instead of hot
water and fat, use buttermilk if you can
get it.

* * *

Rizzered Haddies

Fresh haddocks · butter · salt

You will need medium sized freshly caught fish. Gut, wipe, salt and leave overnight. Thread a wire through the eye sockets and hang up for two or three days in the open air, but not in the sun. Now skin and bone them, and broil lightly brown on a gridiron. Serve hot with melted butter.

* * *

Soda Scones

1 lb flour · ¾ tsp bicarb. soda · ½ tsp salt · ½ tsp tartaric acid · buttermilk

Mix the dry ingredients and add buttermilk to make a very soft dough. Roll out about ½" thick on a floured board. Using a plate for template, cut out two rounds, & cut

across into six scones. Fire on a medium
hot floured girdle for about ten minutes,
turn and do the remaining side.

*   *   *

Parritch

1 pint water · 1 handful oatmeal · 1 tsp salt

Bring the water to a fast boil, add the salt
and slowly sprinkle in the oatmeal,
stirring all the time to prevent knots.
Simmer for 30 minutes, stirring regularly.
Serve hot on a cold plate, with a cup of
fresh milk or cream. Use medium, not
fine oatmeal. If you cannot spare 30
minutes in the morning, leave the oatmeal
soaking in the pan overnight. In the
morning all you have to do is bring it to
the boil and keep it there about 3 minutes,
stirring all the time.

*   *   *

23

Nettle Broth

1 lb young nettle tops · 3 oz barley · chicken stock · salt · pepper

Gather fresh young nettle tops, wash well in salted water and chop finely. Add to the boiling stock with the barley, simmer until tender. Add salt and pepper to taste. Should thickening be desirable, add some mashed potatoes.

* * *

Athole Brose

1 lb heather honey · 3 oz oatmeal · 1½ pints whisky · 1 cup water

Mix the water and oatmeal, then press all the liquid through a fine sieve. Dissolve the honey in this and add the whisky. Whisk well together, then bottle. Store in a cool place . Shake well before serving .

* * *

Tatties an' Herrin'

Fresh herring · potatoes · salt & water

Take enough scrubbed potatoes to nearly fill
the pot, add salt and water and bring to
the boil . Pour off most of the water when
the potatoes are half done, and return the
pot to the stove. Lay your cleaned herring
on top of the potatoes, replace the lid tightly,
and allow to cook in the steam . When ready,
remove the fish & keep hot while the potatoes
are kept steaming until dry and mealy .

* * *

Powsowdie

1 sheep's head · 1½ lbs mixed vegetables · 4oz barley · 3 quts water · 2 tblsp fine oatmeal · 2 tblsp parsley · pepper · salt

Thoroughly singe the sheep's head. At one time this was done at the forge of the local smiddy. Brush well, put in a pot & cover with salted water. Leave over night. Next day, bring to boil and simmer for 1 hour, skimming several times. Add your chopped & diced vegetables [peas, potatoes, leeks, carrots, turnips, onions – whatever is in season]. Stir in the oatmeal and barley. Simmer another 30 minutes, & season to taste. Continue to simmer for another 30 minutes. Add chopped parsley just before serving.

* * *

Sheep's Heid Broth

Another name for Powsowdie. Head is not singed first.

Selkirk Bannock

2 lbs flour · 1 lb sultanas · ½ lb sugar · 4oz butter · 4oz
lard · 4oz candied peel · ½ pt milk · 1oz yeast · ¼ tsp salt

Cream the yeast with some sugar in warm
water, melt the fats in warm milk, and add
together. Mix into the flour the sultanas,
sugar, chopped peel & salt, then add the milk
& fats. Leave to rise about double its bulk
in a warm place, about 60 minutes. Knead
well, place in a greased tin, which it should
only half fill, and again leave to rise. Then
bake in a moderate oven for up to 1½ hours.
Glaze the top by brushing with sweetened milk
30 minutes before you take it from the oven.
The top should be a golden brown, but test
with a skewer to make sure that the inside
has been properly cooked.

* * *

27

Rowan Jeely

Fresh rowan berries · sugar · water

Pick fresh rowan berries and put into a brass preserving pan with just enough water to cover them. Simmer very slowly, stirring with a wooden spoon, until the berries are soft. Strain through a jelly bag. To each pint of juice add 1 lb sugar, and boil until it jells. This will take 30 minutes or more. If too tart for your taste, more sugar may be added.

*   *   *

Mashlam Scones

4oz flour · 4oz fine oatmeal · 1oz butter · 1 tsp sugar. ¾ tsp baking powder. ½ tsp cream of tartar. pinch of salt · buttermilk

Sieve together the dry ingredients, then

rub in the butter. Add enough buttermilk
to make a light dough. Knead quickly on
a floured board, & make a round. Bake on hot girdle.

* * *

A Fitless Cock *

1 egg · 4oz oatmeal [medium] · 2 oz suet · 1 onion · salt · pepper

Chop the onion very finely, mix with the other
dry ingredients and bind with the beaten
egg. Shape the mixture like a trussed fowl
and tie up in a well scalded cloth. Boil
for two hours. May be served with meat or
on its own.

* * *

* "Fit" is a foot, so a fitless cock is a footless cock

29

Oatmeal Soup

1 pint chicken stock · 1 onion · 2 tblsp oatmeal · ½ pint
milk · ¼ pint cream · parsley · pepper &
salt · 1 large knob of butter

Chop a large onion finely, fry lightly in
the butter, add oatmeal and seasoning
and continue several minutes. Add this
to the chicken stock and heat, stirring all
the time till it boils. Replace the lid and
simmer for about 30 minutes. Pass through
a sieve and add the warmed milk.*Add the
chopped parsley a few minutes before serving.
Pour a swirl of cream on top of each plateful.

* * *

* Reheat.

Paisley Almond Cakes

2 oz rice flour · 2 oz cornflour · 3 oz caster sugar · 3 oz butter ·
1½ oz ground almonds · 1 level tsp baking soda ·
2 eggs · pinch of salt

Mix together the flour and baking soda. Cream the butter and sugar, and beat the eggs. Taking small amounts of flour and egg in turn, beat into the creamed butter and sugar, and when smooth, mix in the ground almonds with a small pinch of salt. Grease a dozen patty tins and half fill with the mixture. Bake for 10-15 minutes in a moderate oven, then turn out to cool on a wire rack.

* * *

Partan Bree

1 large crab · 2–3 oz rice · 1 pint white stock · 1 pint
milk · ½ pint cream · anchovy paste · salt & pepper

Remove all the meat from your crab, but
put aside the claw meat. Boil the rice
until it is soft enough to pass through a
sieve with the crab meat. Stir until smooth,
adding the white stock. Add anchovy &
season, then heat in the pan without letting
it boil. Stir all the time, and add the
claw meat. Just before serving, lace in
half a pint of cream.

* * *

Dundee Cake

12 oz s/r flour · 8oz butter · 8oz sugar · 4oz each, currants,
raisins, sultanas, peel · 3 oz split almonds · 3 oz gr. almonds.
grated rind of lemon · 4 eggs · 1 tsp milk · pinch of salt

32

Cream together the butter and sugar, then beat in the eggs and flour with a pinch of salt. Stir in the dried fruits, lemon rind & ground almonds. Put into a greased cake tin lined with greased paper and bake in a moderate oven 2½ – 3 hours. A piece of paper on top will prevent scorching. When half cooked, sprinkle the split almonds on top, removing the paper. A few minutes before taking the cake from the oven, brush over with sweetened milk to glaze it. The cake should be allowed to cool in the tin.

* * *

Colcannon

Potatoes · cabbage · butter · salt · pepper

This requires equal quantities of boiled potatoes and cabbage. Mash the potatoes and chop the cabbage, then add about one ounce of melted butter to the pound, mix well

and season to taste. Serve very hot. A
variation is to put the mixture in a
greased pie dish and brown in the oven.
Grated cheese may be sprinkled over the top.

*　　*　　*

Cullen Skink

1 smoked haddock · 1 pint milk · 1 onion · 1 oz butter ·
mashed potato · salt and pepper

The fish should preferably be a Finnan Haddy.
Skin and place in a pan with just enough
water to cover, and bring to the boil. Add
the chopped onion, and when the fish is
cooked, remove from the pan & take out
all the bones. These are returned to the
stock & boiled one hour. Strain & bring
again to the boil, adding the flaked fish
with the boiling milk. Season to taste, add
enough mashed potato to give it consistency,
add small pieces of butter & serve hot.

*　　*　　*

Whisky Punch

1 bottle whisky · 2 pints water · 3 lemons · 8oz sugar

Finely peel three large lemons, squeeze out
the juice, and put all in a bowl with 8oz
of sugar. Brown or Demerara for preference.
Pour on two pints of boiling water, and
when cold, strain and mix in a bottle
of whisky. Serve well chilled.

* * *

Crappit Heid

4 haddock heads · 4 haddock livers · oatmeal · milk · salt

Mix together equal amounts of chopped livers
and oatmeal. Season and add a little milk
to bind, then stuff the heads with the
mixture. Butter a stewpan and put in
the heads standing on end. Pour over
them some fish stock. Stew gently for

35

around thirty minutes. Serve very hot.

* * *

Roastit Bubblyjock

1 10-12 lb turkey · 1 lb sausage meat · ¼ lb dripping · 2 oz butter · 1 pint giblet stock · salt · pepper · 1 tblsp cranberry jelly · STUFFING: 4 oz breadcrumbs · 2 oz suet · 10 chestnuts · turkey liver · 1 tsp chopped parsley · ¼ tsp mixed herbs · milk · salt and pepper

Prepare the stuffing by first soaking the breadcrumbs in a little milk, then mixing with the other ingredients. Stuff the bird with this and skewer closed. Stuff the crop opening with the sausage meat, and close in the same way. Now put the turkey in a roasting tin with the dripping, and brush all over with melted butter. Roast in a slow oven, allowing about 25 minutes per pound, and baste regularly. Pour off surplus fat from the roasting tin when

the turkey is cooked, add the pint of giblet
stock and the cranberry jelly and boil quickly
to thicken the sauce. Serve separately.

* * *

Ballater Scones

1 lb flour · 3 oz butter · ½ pint tepid milk · 1 tsp baking soda ·
2 tsp cream of tartar · salt

Add a pinch of salt to the flour and baking
soda and cream of tartar, and rub in
the butter. Mix with the tepid milk
and knead to a stiff dough. Roll out
about half an inch thick on a floured
board. Cut in rounds with a scone cutter,
and bake in a hot oven. When nearly
done, brush with milk, and finish
baking. Serve hot, split open and
buttered well.

* * *

Hodgils

Oatmeal · chives · beef broth · salt & pepper

Chop some chives finely and add to one
or two handfuls of medium oatmeal.
Season to taste. Take some of the fatty
top of the broth to moisten and bind.
Put into the boiling broth and cook for
twenty minutes.

* * *

Black Bun

2 lbs currants · 1 lb muscatels · 1 lb sultanas · 1 lb flour ·
½ lb sugar · ½ lb mixed peel · ½ lb almonds · ½ oz cinnamon ·
½ oz ground ginger · 1 tsp allspice · ½ tsp black pepper ·
1 tsp baking soda · 2 tblsp brandy · 1 beaten egg · milk ·
CASE: 1 lb flour · ½ lb butter · 2 oz sugar · pinch of salt

Mix well together all the ingredients but the
milk, then add just enough to moisten.

Spoon into the pastry lined tin, making it
slightly higher in the centre, then cover
the top with pastry. Damp the edges and
pinch to make sure it holds. Prick all over
with a fork, then brush over with beaten
egg. Bake in a slow oven for 3 hours, and
test with a thin skewer. The case pastry is
made by rubbing the flour and butter
finely together, adding the salt and sugar,
then enough cold water to make a stiff dough.
Roll out thinly on a floured board, and line
a suitable tin, keeping a large enough round
for the top.

* * *

Crullas

1 lb flour · 4 eggs · 4 oz sugar · 4 oz butter · 1 tsp baking
powder · ½ tsp salt · ½ tsp cream of
tartar · buttermilk

Cream together the butter and sugar. Mix

in the rest of the ingredients, adding the
buttermilk last in just sufficient
quantity to make a stiff dough. Roll out
thinly on a floured board, and cut into
strips about an inch wide. Plait three
together, about six inches long, damping
the ends & pinching them together. Fry
golden in hot fat, drain, and dredge with
caster sugar.

* * *

Skirlie

½ lb oatmeal · ½ lb grated suet · 2 onions · pepper · salt

Toast the oatmeal before the fire or in the
oven. Use the medium grade. Brown the
chopped onions in the suet, add the oatmeal
and seasoning and fry till brown. Keep
stirring all the time.

* * *

Pitcaithly Bannock

14 oz flour · 2 oz rice flour · 10 oz butter · 4 oz sugar · 2 oz
mixed peel · 2 oz chopped almonds

Knead well all the ingredients. No moistening
is required. Put in two round flat tins,
decorate the edges with the finger or end
of a soup spoon. Prick all over and bake
in a slow oven for about half an hour.

* * *

Chicken Stovies

3 lb chicken · 3 onions · 2 oz butter · 1 pint stock · 2½ lb
potatoes · 2 tblsp chopped parsley · salt

Cut the chicken in pieces, and brown lightly
in half the butter. Remove from the pan,
and fill with alternate layers of sliced
potato, sliced onion and chicken, seasoning
as you go, and dotting with butter.

Finish with a layer of potatoes, and pour
in the giblet stock . Replace lid tightly
and simmer for 2½ hours, checking
occasionally to see it does not dry up.
Sprinkle with parsley before serving .

* * *

Scotch Broth

2 lb neck of mutton · 3 oz peas · 2 oz pot barley · 1 large
onion · 1 large leek · ½ small cabbage · 3 oz turnip · 3 oz
carrot · 3 oz grated carrot · 1 tblsp chopped parsley · salt
and pepper · 2 quts water

Trim the meat and put in a pot of cold
water with peas, barley and seasoning.
[Dried peas should be soaked overnight.]
Bring to the boil and skim . Slice the leek
and onion, dice the turnip and carrot, add
and simmer for 3 hours . Then add the
grated carrot and shredded cabbage, and
simmer another 30 minutes . Shortly

before serving add in the chopped parsley.
Serve very hot.

*   *   *

Pan Haggerty

1 lb potatoes · ½ lb onions · 3 oz grated cheese · 2 oz fat ·
salt · pepper

Slice the potatoes and onions finely, heat the
fat in the frying pan, and put in
alternate layers of each, sprinkling with
cheese, and seasoning each layer. Fry
slowly, and when cooked, brown under
the grill.

*   *   *

Cock-a-Leekie

3 lb boiling fowl · 1 dozen leeks · 1 dozen cooked prunes.
sprig parsley · salt & pepper

Simmer the fowl, covered with water in a
closed pot for 2 to 3 hours. Add the leeks,
cut small, with the prunes and chopped
parsley, and boil for another 45 minutes.
A good pinch of sugar may also be added.
Serve very hot.

* * *

Taiblet

4 lbs caster sugar · 1 lb sweetened condensed milk [tinned].
½ lb butter · 1 pint water

Melt the butter in hot water in a deep pan,
add the sugar, then bring to the boil,
keeping it stirred. When it boils, add the
tin of milk and simmer about 30 minutes.

44

Remove pot from the stove, add flavouring
& colouring if wanted, and beat thoroughly
for 5 minutes or so while it cools. Grease
a flat tin, pour in the mixture, and when
set but not cold, cut into bars with a knife.

*   *   *

Pancakes

½ lb s/r flour · 3 oz sugar · 2 eggs · milk · pinch of salt

Beat the eggs, then beat into the flour, salt,
and sugar. Add sufficient milk to
make a quick dropping batter. Take
large spoonfuls and drop on a hot
greased girdle. Brown lightly golden
on both sides, and put on a towel
to cool.

*   *   *

Brandy Snaps

3 oz flour · 3 oz butter · 3 oz sugar · 3 oz syrup · 1 tsp ginger

Grease your baking trays with butter.
Heat the butter, sugar and syrup in a pan
until melted, then allow to cool a little.
Mix in the flour and ground ginger, and
while still warm drop teaspoons of the
mixture on the trays, being careful to leave
plenty of room for spreading. Bake until
golden in a moderate oven, then take out
and allow to cool for a short while. Lift with
a broad knife & wrap round the greased
handle of a spurtle or wooden spoon. When
they have set, fill with brandy flavoured
whipped cream.

* * *

Barley Scones

2 cups barley flour · knob of butter · 3/4 tsp cream of
tartar · ½ tsp baking powder · buttermilk ·
pinch of salt

Rub the butter into the mixed dry ingredients.
Make into a soft dough with buttermilk.
Roll out into a round about ¼" thick.
Bake on a hot girdle, & turn over to cook
the other side.

* * *

Sauty Bannocks

6 oz oatmeal · 1 egg · 1 pt milk · 1 tsp golden syrup · 1 tsp
sugar · ½ tsp salt · ½ tsp bicarbonate of soda

Take the dry ingredients, put in a bowl and
mix together. Dissolve the syrup in the milk,
add and leave overnight. Next day add
the beaten egg. If it is too thick, add more

milk to make a pouring consistency.
Pour on a hot girdle, tilting to spread it
more thinly, and bake both sides. Pile
bannocks together to cool, & cover with a
cloth.

* * *

Brose

Medium oatmeal · cream · pinch of salt

Take an appropriate quantity of oatmeal, add
salt and put in a bowl. Pour boiling
water over it, just enough to wet well,
stirring quickly. Allow the oatmeal a few
minutes to swell up, and serve still hot
with cream.

Kale or neep brose is made the same way, but
using the water the vegetables were boiled
in. This may also be served with the
brose instead of the cream.

* * *

Tannielaggie Scones

½ lb flour · 4 oz butter · 1 tblsp sugar · 1 tsp baking soda

Rub the butter into the flour, adding the sugar and baking soda. Add enough water to make a stiff dough. Roll out very thinly, and cut into biscuit sized rectangles. Brown very lightly in a moderate oven until they resemble water biscuits.

* * *

Edinburgh Rock

1 lb sugar · ½ tsp cream of tartar · 1½ gills of water

In a suitable pan, melt the sugar in the water, and bring nearly to the boil. Add the cream of tartar just before boiling point. Boil without stirring until the toffee forms a hard lump in cold water. Take off the stove and add colour & flavouring, then

pour on to a greased marble slab. When
it has cooled enough to handle, sprinkle
with icing sugar, and repeatedly "pull"
until it is dull & opaque. Pull out into
long thin strips, and with a pair of greased
scissors cut into 6" lengths. Leave in a
warm room for a day or so until the rock
becomes powdery & brittle, when it can be
stored in an air tight tin or jar.

* * *

Barley Bannocks

8 oz flour · 8 oz barley meal · 1 large tsp each of salt &
cream of tartar · 1 tsp baking soda · milk

Add enough milk to the mixed dry ingredients
to make a softish dough. Knead lightly
on a floured board, and make into a round
bannock about 2" deep. Prick all over,
and bake in a moderate oven about 1 hour.

* * *

Mutton Hams

10 lb leg of mutton · 1 lb brown sugar · 1½ lbs sea salt ·
2 oz allspice · 2 oz saltpetre · 1 oz peppercorns · 1 oz coriander
seed · 8 juniper berries · 8 pints water

Put all the ingredients in a large pot, bring to
the boil, and boil for five minutes. When
cool, strain into a suitable container, & leave
the meat, covered by the liquid, for two weeks.
The container should be covered, and the
room temperature should not reach 60°.
Thoroughly wash the meat when you remove
it from the brine, and soak in cold water
for 3 – 4 hours. Smoke the meat over a
peat or oak chip fire for up to two weeks.
Allow 30 minutes per pound when cooking
the meat. Cover with cold water, add
suitable vegetables, and bring to the boil.
This method may also be used for beef and
pork, or ducks and geese. Allow any meat
to cool in the stock when serving cold.

* * *

Burnmouth Gless Candy

1 lb sugar · 2 tblsp vinegar · 1 cup water

Put all the ingredients in a pan, bring to
the boil, and boil without stirring until
a sample cracks when tried in cold water.
This toffee is clear like glass, and may be
used for toffee apples, nuts etc. Colouring
may be added for a change.

* * *

Crowdie

1 quart milk · ¼ tsp rennet · salt

Slowly heat the milk to just over 70°, and
stir in the rennet. Leave to cool and
set. Cut up into cubes. When the whey
rises, strain off through a sieve, tie up the
curd in a muslin & hang up for 1 hour. Add salt.

* * *

Kale Brose

Piece of ox head or hough · 1 curly kale · 1 cup oatmeal ·
salt & pepper

Boil the meat in salted water until the fat is
freed. Take a plant of curly kale - at its
best after a touch of frost – and wash
carefully. Shred small and boil 10-15
minutes in the stock. Put the lightly
toasted oatmeal in a bowl & add salt to taste.
On it pour a cupful of top of the stock, with
plenty of fat in it. Stir until "knotty", then
return to the pot, and after taking out
the meat, boil another two or three minutes.
Serve hot.

* * *

Broonie

6 oz flour · 6 oz medium oatmeal · 4 oz sugar · 2 oz butter ·
1 egg · 2 tblsp treacle · buttermilk · 1 tsp baking soda ·
1 tsp ground ginger · salt

Mix together the dry ingredients, using just
a pinch of salt, and not too much baking
soda. Rub in the butter. Heat the treacle
to make it more fluid, and mix in the beaten
egg with a little buttermilk. Mix this
in with the flour, adding enough buttermilk
to make a dropping consistency. Pour
into a greased loaf tin, and bake in a
moderate oven 1¼ hours. Allow to cool
in the tin for a while when baked, and
put on a wire rack to finish cooling overnight.
This is an orkney gingerbread.

* * *

Clootie Dumplin'

2 lbs flour · ½ lb suet · ½ lb sugar · ½ lb raisins · ½ lb
currants · 1 lb treacle · 1 cup breadcrumbs · 1 egg
2 tsp cream of tartar · 2 tsp baking soda

Mix together all the ingredients with enough
buttermilk to make a soft dough. Take
a pudding cloth out of boiling water and
wring dry. Dredge with flour, put in a
pudding basin, and put in the mixture.
Tie the top of the cloth together, leaving room
for the dumpling to swell. Put into a pot
of boiling water, which should cover the
dumpling easily. Simmer for 3 hours. Check
occasionally in case you need to top up with
more boiling water. Turn out on a plate,
take off the cloth, and dry out the outside
in the oven. Sieve over with caster sugar,
and serve with hot sauce. It can also
be eaten cold, sliced; or re-heated, fried.

*　*　*

Fife Bannocks

6 oz flour · 4 oz medium oatmeal · 1 oz butter · pinch
of salt & sugar · ¾ tsp cream of tartar · ½ tsp baking
soda · buttermilk

Mix together the dry ingredients, then rub
in the butter. Add milk to make a light
dough. Knead lightly on a floured board,
and roll out into a round. Cut in four
& bake on a hot girdle, or in a hot oven.

*   *   *

Caledonian Cream

1 lb crowdie or curds · 2 tblsp sugar · 2 tblsp marmalade ·
2 tblsp whisky · 1½ tblsp lemon juice

Mix together all the ingredients. Whisk
thoroughly and freeze.

*   *   *

Blawn Whitings

Fresh whitings · sea salt

ake very fresh fish, and clean and gut as
soon as possible. Skin and remove the eyes.
Cover with salt, & rub it well in along the
inside of the fish. Shake off surplus salt,
put a string or wire through the eye sockets
and hang up outside to blow in a fresh breeze,
but out of direct sun. Alternatively, hang
up under cover, but where there is always
a current of air. Small whitings may be
cooked next morning, but large ones may
need perhaps two more days. Roll lightly
in flour and broil over a slow heat. Serve
very hot, with melted butter.

* * *

Ayrshire Shortbread

1 lb flour · 9 oz butter · 2 egg yolks · 5 oz sugar · 2-3 drops vanilla essence

Knead well together all the ingredients into a dryish crumbly texture. Put into round flat tins, decorate round the edges with a spoon handle, prick all over, and bake for half an hour in a slow oven.

* * *

Potted Hough

3 lb hough joint · salt and pepper

Put the joint in a pot, cover with water and simmer 3 - 4 hours. Strain, and then mince the meat, fine or rough as you prefer. Add to the stock, season, and boil a further 10 minutes. Leave to set in moulds. Use cold.

* * *

Shetland Bride's Bonn

8 oz flour · 4 oz butter · 2 oz sugar · 1 tsp caraway seed

Rub the butter into the flour and sugar,
adding the caraway seed. Use a small
amount of milk to make a scone dough.
Pat into a round and fire both sides on
the girdle.

*   *   *

Queen Mary's Tart

8 oz flour · 6 oz butter · ¼ tsp salt · FILLING: 2 oz butter.
2 oz sugar · 2 oz candied peel · 2 beaten eggs · 1 large
dessert spoon sultanas

Make a puff pastry in the usual way with
the flour, butter & salt. Butter a plate or
flan tin and line with this. Bake for 30 to
40 minutes after filling with the fruit mixture. Hot oven.

*   *   *

Parkins

1 lb oatmeal · 1 lb flour · ¾ lb demerara sugar · ½ lb
butter · 2 eggs · 4 tblsp syrup · 3 tsp baking soda · 2 tsp
cinnamon · 1 tsp ginger · 1 tsp spice

Rub the butter into the mixed dry ingredients.
Add the beaten eggs and syrup to make
a fairly stiff dough. Roll into small pieces,
about the size of a walnut. Put on greased
tins with a split almond on top of each
and bake in a moderate oven.

* * *

Jenny Neil's Sandwich

¼ lb s/r flour · ¼ butter · ¼ lb sugar · 3 fresh eggs

Cream the butter & sugar, then gradually
beat in the flour and eggs. Bake in
sandwich tins for 20 minutes in a moderate
oven. Turn out to cool on a wire rack.

* * *

Lang Kale

Curly kale · oatmeal · cream · sugar · seasoning

Cut away the central ribs from your curly kale,
and put the leaves in a pot with boiling
water. Boil quickly till tender, strain and
chop finely. Sprinkle with toasted oatmeal
& return to the pot. Add the cream [or
butter], sugar, just a pinch, and seasoning.
Stir well and boil a few more minutes.
Use as small an amount of water as possible.

* * *

Oatmeal Biscuits

*10 oz oatmeal · 10 oz flour · 4oz butter · 4oz sugar · 1 egg ·
1 tsp baking soda · milk · pinch salt*

Mix the oatmeal and flour and rub in the
butter. Add the sugar, salt and baking
soda. Beat the egg and add. Use enough

milk to make a stiff dough. Roll out
thinly on a floured board, cut into rounds
and bake in a moderate oven until crisp

*   *   *

Butterscotch

2 lbs sugar · ½ lb butter · pinch of salt

Heat the sugar in a pan and when it melts
add the salt and butter. Bring to the
boil, stirring all the time, and continue
until it hardens when tested in cold water.
Pour into a buttered tin. When it starts
to cool, mark in small squares with a knife.

*   *   *

Potted Herrin'

8 fresh herring · coarse oatmeal · vinegar · salt · pepper

Scale and clean the herring, split open
and remove the backbones. Sprinkle
with salt and pepper, both sides. Roll
up tightly, tails first. Pack the rolls
closely together in a piedish, and add
half an inch of water & vinegar mixed.
Sprinkle liberally with oatmeal, and
cook in a moderate oven about 40 minutes
till brown and crisp on top.

*   *   *

Scotch Eggs

1 lb sausage meat · 7 eggs · breadcrumbs · salt · pepper

Hard boil six eggs and beat the other.
Cool and shell the eggs. Divide the sausage
meat into six, and flatten each piece.

Dip each hard boiled egg in beaten egg,
and cover evenly with sausage meat. Roll
each in beaten egg and cover with bread
crumbs. Fry in deep fat until brown.

*   *   *

Index